Dedicated To:
Gentlemen & Grandad

Written by: Abigail Gartland

Hello, my name is St. Padre Pio!

I was born in Italy in 1887!

When I was only five years old, I decided that I was going to be a priest!

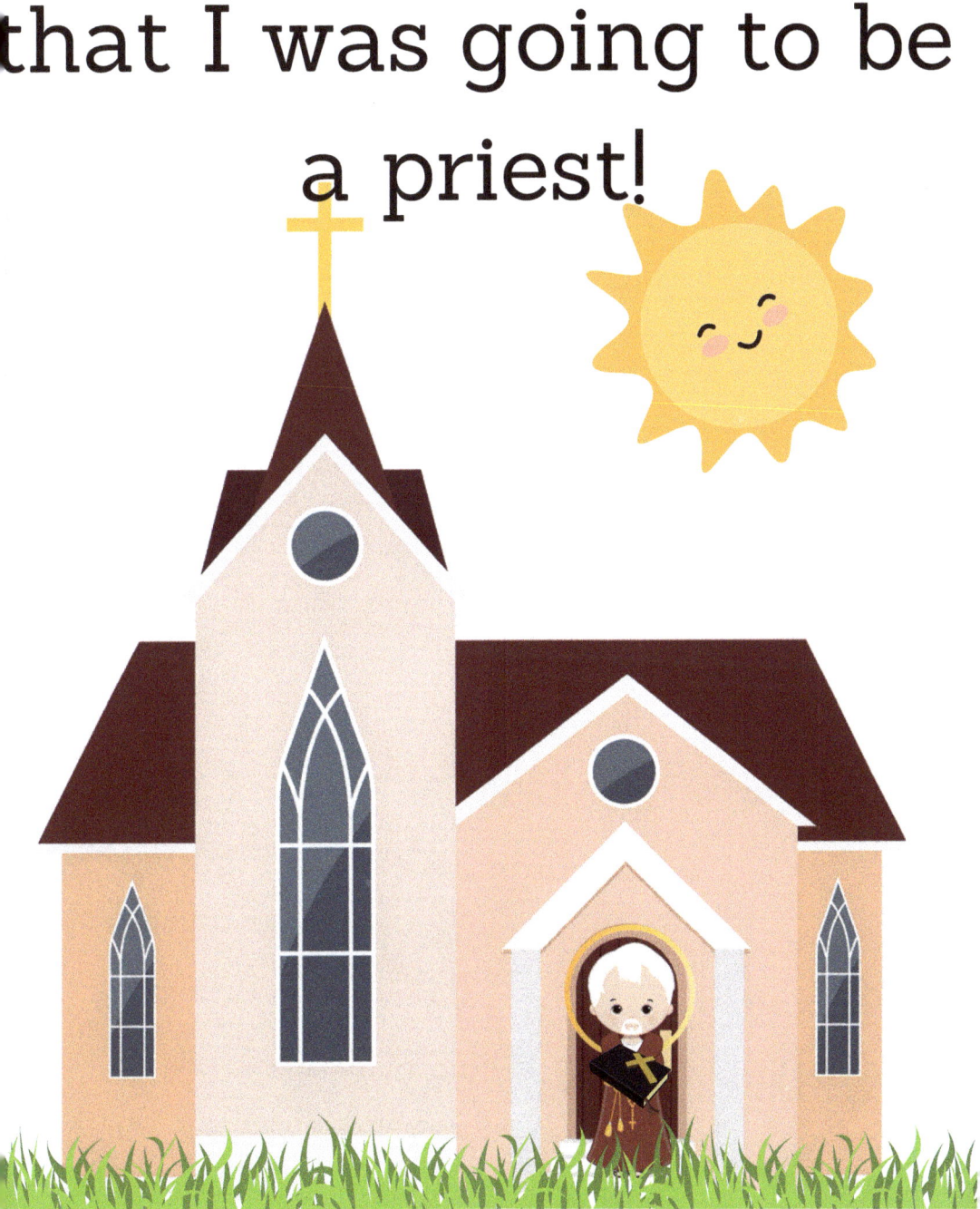

When I was young, I could see Jesus and Mary. I loved to see them!

could also see others' guardian angels who were protecting people.

When I grew up, I became a priest.

One day I was hearing confessions, and my hands and feet started to hurt.

I noticed that my hands and feet looked like Jesus' when he died.

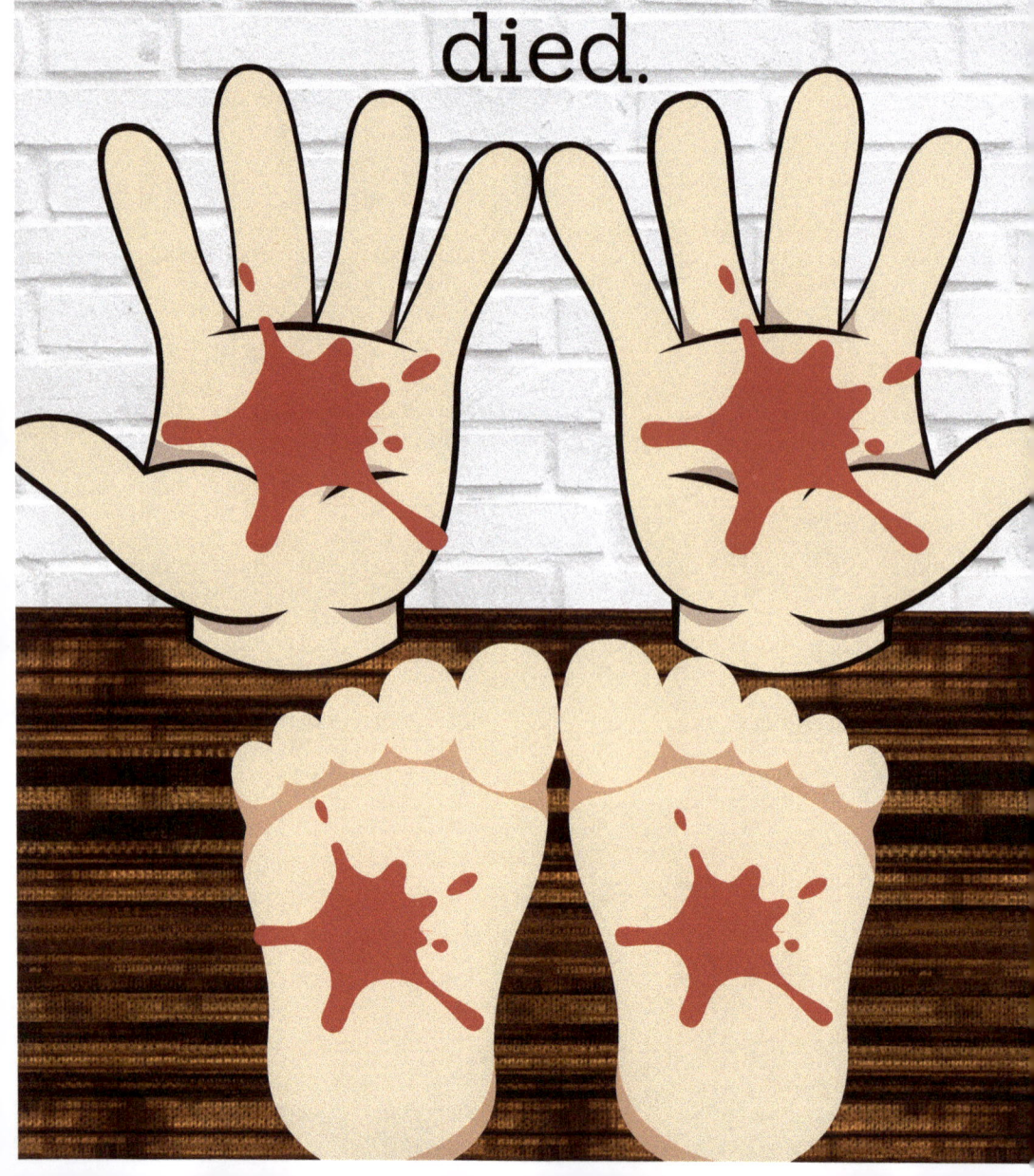

I suffered, but this meant that Jesus was very close to me.

People came from all around the world to see me.

I am the patron saint of kids, and people who are nervous.

Do you want to be more like me?

First, you can celebrate my feast day with me on September 23rd!

Second, you can always ask Jesus and Mary to keep you safe.

One of my favorite things to say is "Pray, Hope and Don't Worry!"

pray for you every day of your life.

St. Padre Pio Pray for us!

opyright:

ipart: © PentoolPixie © LimeandKiwiDesigns
censed purchased: 1/10/2024

About the Author

Abigail Gartland

I love the saints and I love my faith. The idea for sharing the stories of the saints with little ones came when my dear friends were expecting their first baby. I wanted to create something as unique and special as our friendship. Each book is dedicated to very special people and groups who have enriched my faith in different ways. I am blessed to write these stories and appreciate the unending support of my family and friends. When I am not writing, am a middle school teacher. I hope you enjoy these stories. I pray for each and every person who opens one of my books to learn more about the saints.

Abbie

www.ingramcontent.com/pod-product-compliance
Lightning Source LLC
LaVergne TN
LVHW051043070526
838201LV00067B/4904